CHILDREN'S STORYTELLERS

Dav Pilkey

by Chris Bowman

BLASTOFF! READERS
4

BELLWETHER MEDIA • MINNEAPOLIS, MN

Note to Librarians, Teachers, and Parents:

Blastoff! Readers are carefully developed by literacy experts and combine standards-based content with developmentally appropriate text.

Level 1 provides the most support through repetition of high-frequency words, light text, predictable sentence patterns, and strong visual support.

Level 2 offers early readers a bit more challenge through varied simple sentences, increased text load, and less repetition of high-frequency words.

Level 3 advances early-fluent readers toward fluency through increased text and concept load, less reliance on visuals, longer sentences, and more literary language.

Level 4 builds reading stamina by providing more text per page, increased use of punctuation, greater variation in sentence patterns, and increasingly challenging vocabulary.

Level 5 encourages children to move from "learning to read" to "reading to learn" by providing even more text, varied writing styles, and less familiar topics.

Whichever book is right for your reader, Blastoff! Readers are the perfect books to build confidence and encourage a love of reading that will last a lifetime!

This edition first published in 2018 by Bellwether Media, Inc.

No part of this publication may be reproduced in whole or in part without written permission of the publisher. For information regarding permission, write to Bellwether Media, Inc., Attention: Permissions Department, 5357 Penn Avenue South, Minneapolis, MN 55419.

Library of Congress Cataloging-in-Publication Data

Names: Bowman, Chris, 1990- author.
Title: Dav Pilkey / by Chris Bowman.
Description: Minneapolis, MN : Bellwether Media, Inc., 2018. | Series:
    Blastoff! Readers: Children's Storytellers | Includes bibliographical
    references and index. | Audience: Grades 2-5
Identifiers: LCCN 2016055097 (print) | LCCN 2017013266 (ebook) | ISBN
    9781626176478 (hardcover : alk. paper) | ISBN 9781681033778 (ebook)
Subjects: LCSH: Pilkey, Dav, 1966–Juvenile literature. | Authors,
    American–20th century–Biography–Juvenile literature. | Children's
    stories–Authorship–Juvenile literature.
Classification: LCC PS3566.I51115 (ebook) | LCC PS3566.I51115 Z56 2018
    (print) | DDC 813/.54 [B] –dc23
LC record available at https://lccn.loc.gov/2016055097

Editor: Betsy Rathburn   Designer: Josh Brink

Printed in the United States of America, North Mankato, MN.

Table of Contents

Who Is Dav Pilkey?	4
Early Adventures	6
Book Number Won	10
Creating Silly Stories	12
Friendship and Fun	16
Lots of Laughter	20
Glossary	22
To Learn More	23
Index	24

Dav Pilkey is an award-winning author and **illustrator**. He is the creator of the popular Captain Underpants **series**. He has also written under the **pen name** Sue Denim.

! fun fact

Dav spelled his name "Dave" until high school. He dropped the "e" after his name tag was misspelled when he worked at Pizza Hut.

The Paperboy

Caldecott Honor Medal

Dav's stories are famous for their silly humor. They are also known for their artwork. Dav's book *The Paperboy* received a **Caldecott Honor**.

Early Adventures

Dav Pilkey was born on March 4, 1966, in Cleveland, Ohio. He grew up with his parents and older sister, Cindy.

"My goal ... was to encourage kids to be creative without worrying about being perfect."
Dav Pilkey

Cleveland, Ohio

N
W E
S

! **fun fact**

Dav usually comes up with a book's title first. Then he writes the story. The pictures come last.

From a young age, Dav struggled with **ADHD** and **dyslexia**. He often had a hard time in school. Still, he liked picking out books to read. But some adults did not like his reading choices.

Dav enjoyed making others laugh. This often got him in trouble in class. His teacher sent him to a desk in the hallway when he acted up. There, he liked to draw and make up stories.

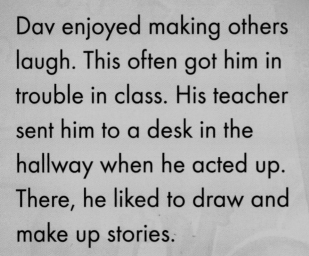

fun fact

Dav started making comic books in second grade. He created Captain Underpants after his teacher said "underwear" in class.

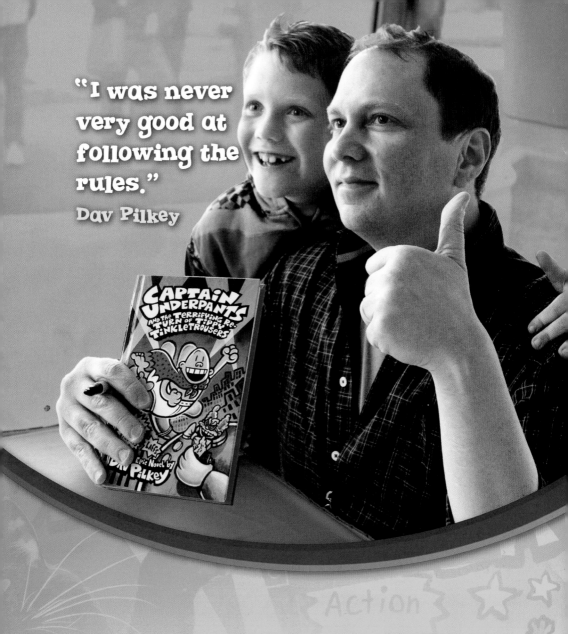

"I was never very good at following the rules."
Dav Pilkey

Dav's teachers did not like his **comics**. But his friends thought they were funny. Dav's parents also encouraged him to keep making more.

Book Number Won

After high school, Dav went to Kent State University to study art. One day, Dav's English teacher saw his drawings. She suggested that he try writing books for children.

Dav wrote a story about a fox and a raccoon and entered it in a contest. He won the prize for his age group! This story became his first book, *World War Won*.

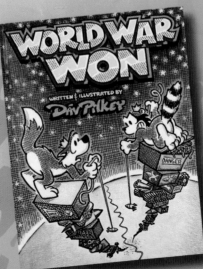

Creating Silly Stories

After finishing school, Dav worked as an artist. He also wrote more books. But Dav had a hard time finding success. His second book was **rejected** 23 times before being **published**!

"I live a very simple life, and often spend several hours each day just daydreaming."
Dav Pilkey

Soon, Dav created the Dragon series. Then he worked on *Kat Kong* and *Dogzilla*. Kids loved these silly stories!

13

Dav did not stop there. Kids enjoyed his
Dumb Bunnies books. *The Paperboy* was
also popular with readers. Then, Dav wrote
a book about a character he created in
second grade. *The Adventures of Captain
Underpants* was a hit!

Today, Dav lives in the **Pacific Northwest** with his wife, Sayuri. They also like to spend time in Japan. Together they like to explore nature and watch movies.

SELECTED WORKS

World War Won (1987)

Dragon series (1991-1993)

Kat Kong (1993)

Dogzilla (1993)

Dumb Bunnies series (1994-1997)

Dog Breath!: The Horrible Trouble with Hally Tosis (1994)

The Paperboy (1996)

Captain Underpants series (1997-)

Ricky Ricotta's Mighty Robot series (2000-)

The Adventures of Ook and Gluk series (2010-)

Dog Man series (2016-)

Dav writes with the same silly humor that he had as a kid. He gives characters names like Wedgie Woman, Professor Poopypants, and Super Diaper Baby. He tries to use jokes to reach readers who struggle with other books.

But not everyone has enjoyed Dav's sense of humor. His Captain Underpants books are commonly **censored** or removed from libraries.

POP CULTURE CONNECTION

Captain Underpants hit the big screen in 2017. Stars such as Kevin Hart, Kristen Schaal, and Ed Helms lent their voices to the film.

THE ADVENTURES OF CAPTAIN UNDERPANTS

Action

Thrills

Laffs

THE FIRST EPIC NOVEL BY DAV PILKEY

SCHOLASTIC

Many of Dav's stories are about teamwork.
Friends work together while they go on
adventures. Their creativity often gets them
in trouble. But it also helps them succeed.

Dav's characters, like George and Harold in Captain Underpants, often misspell words. But they always save the day!

Dav has been making readers laugh for 30 years. He recently started a new series called Dog Man. The second book, *Dog Man Unleashed*, came out in late 2016.

"My dream is that a bunch of kids who were inspired by my books will grow up to be great artists and writers and filmmakers."

Dav Pilkey

IMPORTANT DATES

1966: Dav is born on March 4.

1986: *World War Won* wins Dav's age group in the Landmark Editions' National Written & Illustrated by... Awards Contest for Students.

1987: Dav's first book, *World War Won*, is published.

1997: *The Paperboy* receives the Caldecott Honor.

1998: The California Young Reader Medal is awarded to *Dog Breath!: The Horrible Trouble with Hally Tosis*.

2002: *The Adventures of Super Diaper Baby* debuts at #1 on the *New York Times* bestseller list.

2005: Dav marries his wife, Sayuri.

2015: Dav receives the American Booksellers Association Indie Champion Honor Award.

2016: The Milner Award is given to Dav for helping children develop a love for reading.

It is one of many **spin-off** books from the Captain Underpants series. With more than 70 million books in print, Dav continues to teach kids to have fun and be creative!

Glossary

ADHD—a condition that makes it difficult for a person to focus and sit still; ADHD stands for attention deficit/hyperactivity disorder.

Caldecott Honor—an award given each year to the best-illustrated children's books in America; the Caldecott Medal is given to first place and Caldecott Honors are given to the runners-up.

censored—removed or changed because something is considered dangerous or upsetting

comics—cartoons that tell stories

dyslexia—a condition that makes it hard for a person to read, write, and spell

illustrator—an artist who draws pictures for books

Pacific Northwest—an area of the United States that includes Washington and Oregon

pen name—a name used by a writer instead of the writer's real name

published—printed for a public audience

rejected—turned down

series—a number of things that are connected in a certain order

spin-off—a series or book that is based on characters from a different series or book

To Learn More

AT THE LIBRARY

Hicks, Kelli L. *Dav Pilkey*. Mankato, Minn.: Capstone Press, 2014.

Pilkey, Dav. *The Adventures of Captain Underpants*. New York, N.Y.: Scholastic, 2013.

Wheeler, Jill C. *Dav Pilkey*. Minneapolis, Minn.: ABDO Publishing Company, 2013.

ON THE WEB

Learning more about Dav Pilkey is as easy as 1, 2, 3.

1. Go to www.factsurfer.com.

2. Enter "Dav Pilkey" into the search box.

3. Click the "Surf" button and you will see a list of related web sites.

With factsurfer.com, finding more information is just a click away.

Index

artwork, 5
awards, 4, 10
Caldecott Honor, 5
Captain Underpants
  (series), 4, 8, 14, 17,
  19, 21
censored, 17
childhood, 6, 7, 8, 9
Cindy (sister), 6
Cleveland, Ohio, 6
comics, 9
Dog Man (series), 20
Dogzilla, 13
Dragon (series), 13
drawings, 8, 10
Dumb Bunnies (series),
  14
education, 7, 8, 10
family, 6, 9, 15
humor, 5, 16, 17
important dates, 21
Japan, 15
jobs, 12
Kat Kong, 13
Kent State University, 10
Pacific Northwest, 15

Paperboy, The, 5, 14
pen name, 4
pop culture connection,
  17
quotes, 6, 9, 13, 20
Sayuri (wife), 15
selected works, 15
themes, 16, 18, 19
World War Won, 10
writing, 4, 7, 10, 12, 14,
  16

The images in this book are reproduced through the courtesy of: Ilya S. Savenok/ Getty Images, front
cover, pp. 4, 11, 16, 18, 20; Josh Brink, pp. 5 (top, bottom), 10, 12 (left, right), 17, 19; Rob Kim/ Getty
Images, p. 6; Vladitto, p. 6 (background); Jeff Greenberg/ Alamy, p. 7; MBR/ KRT/ Newscom, p. 8; Bob
Daemmrich/ Alamy, pp. 9, 13; RosaIreneBetancourt 9/ Alamy, p. 14.